READY ANSWERS

A Response to the Evangelical and Fundamentalist Critics of The King James Bible

Phil Stringer, Ph.D.

Copyright 2011
By Dr. Phil Stringer

ISBN 978-0-9846553-1-1

Phil Stringer
5846 N. Kimball
Chicago, IL 60659
Phone: (773) 478-6083
Email: philstringer@att.net

Cover Design and Format by:
The Old Paths Publications, Inc.
Cleveland, Georgia, 30528
Email: TOP@theoldpathspublications.com

Contents

I. Do we Have a 1611 King James Bible Today 5

II. After Easter, After Passover! Is Easter a Mistake? 17

III. Should Fundamentalists Trust Bible Translations From Modernist Bible Societies? 27

IV. Is the Modern King James Movement the Product of the Seventh Day Adventist Cult? 39

V. In Defense of Mark 16:9-20   45

DO WE HAVE A
1611 KING JAMES BIBLE TODAY?

DO WE HAVE A 1611 KING JAMES BIBLE TODAY?

HOW MANY CHANGES?

"There have been thousands of revisions of the King James Bible!" "There have been four revisions of the King James Bible." "There have been no revisions of the King James Bible!" "There have been 22,000 changes in the King James Bible since 1611." "There have been 75,000 changes in the King James Bible since 1611." "There have been 421 changes in the King James Bible since 1611." "There haven't been any changes in the King James Bible since 1611." "I hold in my hands a 1611 King James Bible!" "You couldn't read a 1611 King James Bible if you had one."

All of these statements have been made in connection with the modern debate over the King James Bible. All of them are made by people who are recognized as scholars by one group or another. How can such confusion exist about such a simple subject?

DEFINITIONS

Some of the confusion comes because people use the terms "edition," "revision" and "translation" as if they were interchangeable. They are NOT! There are very real differences in the meanings of these words.

EDITIONS

A new edition refers to a literary work in a new form. The form may be new because of any number of external features. The correction of printing errors, changes in spelling, new footnotes, new marginal references, new parallel verse references, a new type size or font, a new cover or new pictures or maps create a new "edition" of the Bible. They do so without changing the words of the Scripture.

REVISIONS

A new revision of Scripture occurs when words are changed but only in a specific, limited fashion. Revisions occur when one word is used to replace another in order to make the meaning clearer. This is usually done because the meaning of the translated word has changed. The term revision is not applicable to a new translation but only when a new word is chosen to convey the same meaning as the original word but in a clearer fashion. Changes can also take place in word order for the same reason.

TRANSLATIONS

A new translation of Scripture takes place when the process of reproducing a word from one language to another takes place. This involves making a decision about what text or texts of Scripture to accept as the original source. It also involves deciding upon a method of translating and rules for translation.

These definitions of edition, revision and translation are compatible with the dictionary definitions. These definitions are also similar to the terminology used in discussing the translation of ancient books like the writings of Josephus and the various Greek historians.

EDITIONS OF THE KING JAMES BIBLE

There have been thousands of editions of the King James Bible. There were seventeen in the first three years after it was published. The primary reasons for new early editions were to correct printing errors, change type styles and to standardized the spelling of English words. Later editions have also focused on reference helps, including footnotes, parallel references, chapter headings, maps, and concordances.

Printing errors were numerous in the early editions. The Royal Printer was fined 300 pounds sterling for leaving out the word "not" in Exodus 20:14. It took a long time to weed out all of the printing errors. Occasionally, a typographical error will still be seen in a modern edition of the Scripture.

REVISIONS OF THE KING JAMES BIBLE

It is commonly accepted that there have been four real revisions of the King James text before the modern era. There are about 22,000 differences between the first 1611 King James printing and the fourth revision in 1769. However, almost all of these are the correction of printing errors and changes in spelling. Only 136 changes involve "revising" a word or phrase.

D. A. Waite writes:

> "The question is, how great were those revisions? How much has the wording changed? That is why I compared the present day Old Scofield King James Version with the original 1611. Some say there are 40,000 to 50,000 changes, and if you listened to them, you would think we don't have anything like the original today.
>
> The changes, though, are largely related to spelling. For instance, take John 9, the account of the man born blind. Now, the word "blind" in verse 1 is

spelled "blinde." It's a change. But is "blind" any different from "blinde?" If that is a change you're talking about, it doesn't affect the ear. Now, in the second verse, "sin" is spelled "sinne." That is a change. Then the word "born" is spelled "borne." But the sound is the same. What I did, was to count only the changes that could be HEARD. And from Genesis to Revelation, did I get 30,000? No, did I get 20,000? No. 1,000? No. I got 421 CHANGES TO THE EAR that could be heard, out of the 791,328 words. Just 421. That is actually one change out of 1,880 words. As for those 421 CHANGES to the ear - most of them were minor, just changes in spelling.

There were ONLY 136 SUBSTANTIAL CHANGES that were different words. The others were only 285 MINOR CHANGES OF FORM ONLY. Of these 285 MINOR CHANGES, there are 214 VERY MINOR CHANGES such as "towards" for "toward,; "burnt" for "burned", "amongst" for "among", "lift" for "lifted", and "you" for "ye." These kinds of changes represent 214 out of the 285 minor changes of form only.

Thus, you're talking about ONLY 136 REAL CHANGES out of 791,328 words.

Many people imply that the KING JAMES BIBLE is completely changed from what they had in 1611, that there are THOUSANDS of differences. You tell them about the MERE 136 CHANGES OF SUBSTANCE plus 285 MINOR CHANGES OF FORM ONLY." (Waite, The Four-fold Superiority of the King James Bible, Bible for Today, 900 Park Ave., Collingswood, NJ 08108).

Most of these changes involve personal pronouns, articles, conjunctions and prepositions. They are a refinement of the wording of the text, and not a substantial word change. A few English words were substituted for words of similar meaning. This was thought to be the best way of presenting the Hebrew and Greek text in English.

Most of the changes are like the following examples: "grinne" to "grin"; "flying" to "fleeing"; "neeged" to "sneezed"; "saveth to" - "and he saveth"; "northwards" to "northward"; and "noondays" to "noonday."

In 1629, a revision was produced by Cambridge University. Dr. Samuel Ward and Dean John Bois, from the original 1611 translating committee, were involved in this revision. It is the 1629 revision that dropped the Apocrypha from its position between the testaments of Scripture.

In 1638, a further revision was done by Cambridge University. Over 80% of the changes made in the King James Bible were made by this time.

In 1762, Dr. Thomas Paris, a professor at Trinity College in Oxford, issued a revision of the King James. In 1769, Dr. Benjamin Blayney, a professor at Oxford University, issued a further revision expanding upon Dr. Paris' work. Almost all of the changes consisted in revising the italicized words. These words had been supplied by the King James translators for the purpose of dealing with the difference in the Hebrew and Greek languages and English. These words were necessary for an accurate translation.

The 1769 Paris - Blayney revision of the 1611 King James Bible is what Bible believers normally refer to as the King James Bible today. The numbers of revisions are so slight that some scholars are not comfortable using the term "revision" to describe it. Instead, they refer to it as an "edition."

A 1769 Paris - Blayney revision of the King James Bible is properly called a 1611 King James Bible because no new translation work has been done and no new textual authority has been introduced. The 1629 and 1638 revisions and the 1762 and 1769 revisions are all properly called the 1611 King James Bible. The 1611 King James Bible was not retranslated for these revisions. This is the way that revisions of translations of all ancient documents are referred to.

COULD YOU READ A 1611 KING JAMES BIBLE IF YOU HAD ONE?

Actually, the author has read two King James Bibles published in 1611. One is in the chapel of Landmark Baptist College in Haines City, Florida. The other is in the chapel of Heritage Baptist University in Greenwood, Indiana. There are also numerous facsimile copies of the King James Bible published in 1611 available. One is in the library at Landmark Baptist College, Haines City, Florida.

These Bibles can be read easily if you remember a few simple rules:

You will sometimes see an "I" where you are used to seeing a "J."

You will sometimes see an "F" where you are used to an "S."

An additional "E" will be added to many words.

You will sometimes see three "S's" where you are used to seeing two "S's."

Vowels are sometimes doubled.

Consonants are sometimes doubled.

Those who claim that you couldn't read an original 1611 if you had one, apparently haven't tried!

ARE THE MODERN ENGLISH TRANSLATIONS NEW REVISIONS?

It is common for modern English translations to claim to be another revision of the 1611 King James Bible. The title page of the Revised Standard Version claims that the RSV is simply a 1952 revision of the King James. However, the Revised Standard Version was clearly based on a new textual authority and different methods and rules of translations. Soon friends and foes of the RSV were calling it what it really was, a new translation.

Most English Bibles that followed the RSV admitted to being new translations of the Bible. The New International Version states that it is a "completely new translation of the Bible." However, new translations were often promoted and marketed as a "revision" of the King James, even when they clearly were not. There was something about identifying yourself with the King James Bible that was clearly good for sales.

In 1979, the New King James Bible was released and it clearly claimed to be a fifth revision of the King James Bible. This claim is seen in the article at the end of the translation entitled "The History of the King James Bible." It is also clearly seen in the title!

However, the first four revisions brought slightly over one hundred textual changes. The New King James Version produced over 60,000. In the United States, 60,000 changes is the number necessary to produce a claim for a copyright to a new translation (for a work the size of the Bible). The Thomas Nelson Company was granted a copyright on this basis. In the copyright office, it is presented as a new translation. For marketing purposes, it is presented as a revision.

The New King James translators also used new textual authorities for some of their changes. This is clearly seen in their own article, "The History of the King James Bible." The New King James Bible is clearly a new translation and the claim that it is a "revision" of the King James Bible is deceptive and misleading.

The 21st Century King James Version of the Holy Bible and the Third Millennium Bible both claim to be revisions of the King James Bible. Both are published by the same publishers in Gary, South Dakota. They reject the claim of the New King James Bible to be just a revision. However, neither publication has found any acceptance among Bible believing fundamentalists. The publishers have placed a great emphasis on restoring the Apocrypha to their editions of the King James Bible.

The New Scofield Reference Bible places word changes in the text of the Scripture. They are marked by marginal notes which give the King James Bible rendering. It is claimed that this is simply a revision consistent with the works of Paris and Blayney. However, the authority for their changes is often a new textual authority and many of their word changes are clearly a new (and different) translation. This is not the kind of revision done previously to the King James Bible.

HAVE THERE BEEN ANY OTHER GENUINE REVISIONS OF THE KING JAMES BIBLE?

A revision was printed by Royal Printers in England in 1806. It is referred to as "The Eyre and Staham" revision. It did not meet a wide reception and was not able to take the place of the 1769 Paris - Blayney revision.

The King James II was published in the United States in 1971 by Jay P. Green. It seems to be an honest attempt at a real revision (not just a cover for a new translation). However, it never found much of an audience and was soon out of print. There has been talk of reprinting it.

There simply has been no demand for a further revision of the King James Bible. The foes of the King James Bible will not settle for a revision. They want a new translation, with the new textual authority and new translation principles and rules. The friends of the King James Bible have watched it withstand attack after attack. Most of them are in no mood for a discussion of further revision.

DON'T WE NEED A NEW REVISION OF THE KING JAMES?

Fundamentalism has fractured as a movement! Endless debate over the doctrines of inspiration, preservation and the role of the King James Bible has split fundamentalism into several camps. A revision done by the faculty of any fundamentalist Bible college or Christian University would immediately be rejected by large segments of fundamentalism. There exists no potential of uniting different factions to support a new revision.

Many great soul winning, separated, fundamentalist churches are booming while using the King James Bible. Everyday vibrant, growing ministries are disproving the notion that the King James Bible is a hindrance to the ministry today. People are being led to Christ from the King James Bible. They are growing and maturing in the faith while using the King James Bible in its present form. Despite the stated desires of some for a revision of the King James Bible, there simply is not a serious grass roots demand for one.

AFTER EASTER, AFTER PASSOVER! IS EASTER A MISTAKE?

AFTER EASTER, AFTER PASSOVER
IS EASTER A MISTAKE?

One of the most consistent attacks on the King James Bible is that the use of the word Easter in Acts 12:4 is an obvious mistake.

"Perhaps there was never a more unhappy, not to say absurd translation than that in our text."
—Adam Clarke on Acts 12:4

"The word Easter should be Passover."
—J.V. McGee on Acts 12:4

"Acts 12:4 in the KJV says Herod was planning 'after Easter' to bring Peter out. The KJV translates this same Greek word as 'Passover' 28 times. This is the only time they translate this Greek word as 'Easter'. Either the translators were wrong 28 times or they are wrong in Acts 12:4. The NASB translates this Greek word as Passover all 29 times.
—Robert Joyner, King James Only, p.14

"The word that the KJV translates as 'Easter' appears 29 times in the New Testament. In each of the other 28 instances the KJV translates the phrase as "the passover." For example, in John 19:14, "And it was the preparation of the passover, and about the sixth hour: and he saith unto the Jews, Behold the King!' And there is no reason for confusion as to what Luke is referring to here, for the preceding verse said, 'Then were the days of unleavened bread.' The days of unleavened bread, of course, were connected with the Passover celebration. Yet in this one place the AV contains the anachronistic term 'Easter.' Luke's reference to the days of 'unleavened bread' makes it clear that he is referring to the Jewish holiday season, not to

some pagan festival that did not become known by the specific term 'Easter' for some time to come."
–James White,
The King James Only Controversy, p. 233

"Some consider the utilization of 'Easter' in place of passover in Acts 12:4 in the KJV to be an implementation of dynamic equivalency."
–Calvin George,
The Battle for the Spanish Bible, p.83

THE PRINCIPLE OF POLYSEMY

"The capacity of a word to have two or more different meanings is technically known as polysemy."
–David Black,
Linguistics for Students of New Testament Greek,
pp. 124-125

Many words or phrases have more than one possible meaning. This is called polysemy. The proper meaning is determined by "context" - the way the words are used in a given situation. In the dictionary several possible definitions for a polysemic word will be listed. The most common definition will be listed first, then the second most common and so forth. Context will often rule out many translations or definitions that are linguistically possible.

Hebrew, Greek and English are polysemic languages. Polysemic languages are often humorous to people with non-polysemic languages (see Russian comedian Yakov Smirnov's famous comedy skit "The Door Is Ajar").

POLYSEMY AND THE BIBLE

There are many places in the Bible where the principle of polysemy and context play an extremely important role in translation and/or interpretation.

In Isaiah 7:14, virgin is one linguistically possible translation for the Hebrew word almah. Another is young maiden. Context requires the use of the word virgin. This is confirmed by the Greek quotation of Isaiah 7:14 in Matthew 1:23. Virgin is the only possible translation for the Greek word parthenos used in Matthew 1:23.

The King James translation uses the word virtue in Mark 5:30, Luke 6:19, 8:46. Most modern translations use the word "power." Either is possible linguistically but the context demands "virtue." There was more than just the power of a magician involved.

The Hebrew word Elohim (or its Aramaic equivalent) can mean God, gods, or judges. As a result, it is translated God when it refers to the Creator God (Genesis 1:1) or gods when it refers to the pagan gods (many times in the Old Testament). Context dictates what the proper translation is. In Psalm 136:2, it is translated two different ways in the same phrase - context demands it. In Exodus 22:28, the word gods clearly refers to human judges (people who tend to think that they are gods).

In Daniel 3:25, one of several translations is linguistically possible; a son of the gods, or a son of God, or the Son of God, or the son of the gods. Context demands that it be the Son of God - or Daniel 3 becomes a nonsense passage (see v. 28).

POLYSEMY AND BIAS

It is in dealing with polysemic words that the personal and theological bias of translators and interpreters becomes very clear. If you don't believe in the virgin birth, it is very tempting to use the term "young woman" in Isaiah 7:14, even though context demands otherwise. If you don't believe in the Deity of Christ, it is very tempting to translate Daniel 3:25 "a son of the gods" - even though context demands otherwise.

If you are gripped by a prejudice against the King James Bible, you are tempted to pick any translation that is linguistically possible just as long at it is different from the King James Bible. A graphic example is Hosea 3:1.

The Hebrew phrase "flagons of wine" could also be translated "cakes of raisins." This is linguistically possible but is a nonsense translation.

God condemns Israel for drunkenness in chapter 1, 2, 4, and 5 of Hosea. He is clearly doing the same in Hosea 3:1! But an anti-KJB bias makes some people willing to grasp at any possible translation as long as it is different from the KJB.

So the Revised Standard Version reads "and love cakes of raisins," the Contemporary English Version reads "and enjoy cakes with fruit." The New American Standard Version reads, "and love raisin cakes," the New World Translation reads, "loving raisin cakes" and the New International Version "and love the sacred raisin cakes." That's right, these modern translations have God condemning Israel for liking raisins. Anything to keep from agreeing with the KJB.

The Living Bible ignores the Hebrew words completely and uses the phrase "turned to other gods and offered them choice gifts." The New King James Version tries to get out of this amazing mess by adding words: "and love the raisin cakes of the pagans." They admit they added the words "of the pagans" by putting them in italics. The New English Bible reads "And loves raisin cakes offered to idols." No reader of the NEB could tell that the last three words were added to the text. Some are so biased against the KJB that they will believe anything that doesn't match the KJB.

The King James translators referred to flagons of wine because the context demanded it.

EASTER AND POLYSEMY

In the New Testament times, the Greek word "pascha (or pasche)" is used to refer to religious holiday feasts. So are its Hebrew and Aramaic equivalents.

Its most common usage in Greek literature was in reference to the pagan feast of Ishtar. This feast was later adopted by the Roman Catholics and the name changed to Easter. The pagan festival of Ishtar had been around for centuries before Rome tried to "Christianize" it. "Easter is nothing else than Astarte, one of the titles of Beltis, the queen of heaven" (Alexander Hislop, The Two Babylons, p. 103).

The second most common usage was in reference to the Jewish feast of the Passover.

The third most common usage referred to a pagan holiday feast in the fall.

The fourth most common usage referred to a pagan feast in December (later adopted by the Roman Catholics as Christmas). Each time the word was used, the context determined which holiday feast it referred to.

According to the New Oxford English Dictionary, the word paschal: (1) relates to Easter, and (2) relates to the Jewish Passover.

According to Webster's Dictionary, the word Easter originally referred to a pagan spring festival almost coincident in the date with the Passover Festival.

The Roman Catholic church tried to merge the pagan holiday of Ishtar with the Jewish Passover to create a new Christian holiday - Easter. This created confusion in the mind of many in the Christian world.

The word pascha is used 29 times in the New Testament. In most early English Bibles, it is translated Easter every time. This was consistent with Catholic usage. Easter is the most common definition of the word in Greek literature.

However, the King James translators did not follow this policy (as they mention on page 11 of their preface).

In 28 of 29 cases the context demands the translation, Passover. The Jewish holiday is clearly in view. They rejected the Catholic idea of always translating the word pascha as Easter. Recognizing the principle of polysemy, they turned to the second most common definition of the word pasche - passover.

However, in one place they retained the word Easter because the Jewish Passover was clearly not being referred to.

The holiday referred to clearly takes place during or after the feast of the unleavened bread (Acts 12:3-4). The days of the unleavened bread take place for the first seven days AFTER the Passover - see Exodus 12; Ezra 6:19-22; II Chronicles 30:15-21; Deuteronomy 16:1-3; Numbers 28:16-17; Leviticus 23:5-6; Joshua 5:10-11.

This holiday feast took place after the Passover–to call it the Passover would clearly be a mistake.

The word pascha could not refer to the holiday feasts in September or December because this "pascha" followed closely after the Passover which took place in April. Practicing the principle of polysemy, considering the immediate context of Acts 12 and the whole context of Scripture, the KJB translators knew exactly which word to pick. Only the pagan festival of Ishtar (Easter) fits the context. Ishtar was celebrated in the spring. They chose the word Easter precisely because Easter is the only possible correct word here. They used Easter because it was the pagan Easter feast in view in this passage. Their scholarship far outshines the scholarship of their critics.

As Sam Gipp writes:

> "Thus we see that it was God's providence which had the Spirit-filled translators of our Bible to correctly translate 'pascha' as 'Easter.' It most certainly did not refer to the Jewish passover. In fact, to change it to 'passover' would confuse the reader and make the truth of the situation unclear."

CONCLUSION

"Another thing we think good to admonish thee of (gentle Reader) that we have not tried ourselves to an uniformity of phrasing, or to an identity of words, as some peradventure would wish that we had done, because they observe, that some learned men somewhere, have been as exact as they could that way. Truly, that we might not vary from the sense of that which we had translated before, if the word signified that same in both places (for there be some words that be not the same sense everywhere) we were especially careful, and made a conscience, according to our duty. But, that we should express the same notion in the same particular word; as for example, if we translate the Hebrew or Greek word once by PURPOSE, never to call it INTENT; if one where JOURNEYING, never TRAVELING; if one where THINK, never SUPPOSE, of one where PAIN, never ACHE; if one where JOY, never GLADNESS, etc. Thus to mince the matter, we thought to savour more of curiosity than wisdom, and that rather it would breed scorn in the Atheist than bring profit to the godly Reader."

–King James Translators,
from the Preface to the King James Bible

SHOULD FUNDAMENTALISTS TRUST BIBLE TRANSLATIONS FROM MODERNIST BIBLE SOCIETIES?

SHOULD FUNDAMENTALISTS TRUST BIBLE TRANSLATIONS FROM MODERNIST BIBLE SOCIETIES?

Isn't "Bible Society" a wonderful sounding name? Names like "Bible Society" and "Bible Translators" stir up warm images of self-sacrificing missionaries translating the Bible for jungle natives who have never heard the Word of God. Yet that is not always the case!

In an article published in the October 16, 1997, issue of Baptists Today, Barclay Newman, the senior translations officer for the American Bible Society, berated Biblical Fundamentalists by claiming that Fundamentalists place a "claustrophobic framework" (p. 6) upon the Scripture. Insinuating that Fundamentalists have a deficient spiritual mentality, Newman writes: 'Unfortunately, the mentality of fundamentalism tends to foster a "claustrophobic framework," a literal, legalistic interpretation which often suffocates scripture and fails to see the "larger picture" for their false notions of masculine superiority."

According to Newman, these "false notions of masculine superiority" are most evident in the Fundamentalist "manipulation of I Timothy 2:9-15 for the exploitation of women by forbidding them equal opportunity for ministry in the churches." Newman claims that Paul's admonitions in I Timothy 2 and I Corinthians 14:34-35 are "not for every situation" and that they "do not prescribe what must be done in every church of every generation." In his conclusion, Newman pleads with his readers not to allow themselves to remain prisoners of "fundamentalism's claustrophobic framework" and "suffocating framework," which would "refuse half of the human race the opportunity for Christian ministry simply because of a certain birth defect by which they were born female."

From David Cloud, (Fundamental Baptist Information Service,) March 30, 1999 writes:

> "The Bible Society of the Netherlands joined an ecumenical alliance of denominations and para-church organizations to launch the "Year with the Bible" project last September. The project's chairman, Coen Boerma, a former staff member of the World Council of Churches, says the goal is to encourage people to read the Bible (Ecumenical News International, September 16, 1998)."

This sounds like an excellent project (apart from the serious textual and translational problems with Bible Society versions today), but upon further analysis it is evident that the Netherlands Bible Society does not believe nor obey the Bible they distribute. In the interview with Ecumenical News International, Boerma further stated that many parts of the Bible, such as its "negative views on women and homosexuals," are not correct because they "do not fit in our lifestyle any more."

Boerma also said that the goal of the project is not to win people to Christ or to gain converts to the churches. "Evangelization is taboo," he said.

Most people are unaware that the goal of the vast majority of Bible Societies is to replace the Received Text and the King James Bible with modernist Bibles and to replace fundamentalism with modernism.

THE EARLY BIBLE SOCIETIES

The early Bible societies were a product of the modern missions movement of the 1700's and 1800's. They extend from the influence of the Great Awakening of the

1700's in Great Britain and the British colonies that became the United States.

In 1698, the Society for the Promotion of Christian Knowledge was begun in Great Britain. Its goal was the distribution of the King James Bible throughout Europe.

In 1709, the Scottish Society for Propagating Christian Knowledge was begun in Scotland. Its goal was spreading the King James Bible and good commentaries around Europe.

In 1750, the Society for the Propagating of Christian Knowledge among the poor was started to distribute the King James Bible and other literature in the inner cities of the United Kingdom.

In 1780, the Naval and Military Bible Society was started for the purpose of distributing the King James Bible to British military personnel.

The British and Foreign Bible Society was begun in 1804. Its purpose was to translate the Bible into the major languages of the world. For the first ten years, all translations were done from the King James Bible. The BFBS had no doctrinal statement. By 1814, both Roman Catholics and Unitarians joined the BFBS. Soon both groups were involved in Bible translation. They stressed translations from Greek and Hebrew rather than the "inferior" King James Bible. By 1831, the Society rejected the idea of opening with prayers to Jesus Christ because they feared offending their Unitarian members.

THE TRINITARIAN BIBLE SOCIETY

Juanita Carey (E.W. Bullinger: A Biography, p.72-74) describes the formation of the Trinitarian Bible Society this way:

> "The second major difficulty arose several years later when it became apparent that the membership of the Society now included large members of Unitarians. Unitarianism, which denies the deity of Christ, had spread rapidly in Europe in the early part of the nineteenth century. Before long, many of the Society's branches (or auxiliaries, as they were called), especially those on the Continent, consisted almost exclusively of Unitarians. The more conservative members of the Society, who believed in the deity of Christ, found this situation unacceptable. Complaints escalated when other Christian societies began to close their memberships to Unitarians, declaring that only "persons professing a belief in the Holy Trinity could be members or governors.
>
> At the same time, it became quite popular in Christian circles to open meetings with prayer. When this question came up within the British and Foreign Bible Society, the leadership refused to commit itself. Certain members, convinced that this was due to fear of offending the Unitarians by public prayer "in the name of Jesus Christ," pressed the question, but to no avail.
>
> Still not quite satisfied with the way in which the "versions' question" had been handled, these members now felt doubly determined to make themselves heard. After a fruitless attempt to voice their opinions in committee, they decided that they

had no recourse but to force the issues of opening prayer and Unitarian membership at the Annual Meeting in May 1831. The gathering erupted into chaos. Old resentments, doctrinal differences, and religious prejudices all finally surfaced. At the end of a stormy five-and-a-half -hour session, the membership voted, by a majority of six to one, to retain the status quo.

On May 20, 1831, the following resolution was passed by a committee formed from those who had been in the minority.

1. That the persons now present do form a Provisional Committee, with power to add to their number, for the purpose of uniting in such measures as may include the British and Foreign Bible Society to reconsider the decision of the late Anniversary General Meeting of that Institution, and to bring about separation in point of Membership from those who do not acknowledge the doctrine of the Holy Trinity.

2. That a society whose exclusive object is to circulate the pure Word of God, containing that Gospel which is the power of God unto salvation to everyone that believeth, must be considered decidedly a Religious Society.

3. That considering the British and Foreign Bible Society to be a Society of the character above described, it is the opinion of this meeting that the deniers of the doctrine of the Holy Trinity cannot consistently be admitted as members of it.

For a number of months, the members of the Provisional Committee attempted to persuade the parent Society to reconsider its policies. By

November 1831, however, it was decided that there were no grounds for reconciliation. A resolution was passed to form a new Bible Society. And so it was that on December 7, 1831, more than two thousand people gathered at Exeter Hall in London to found a new Society and very explicitly to affirm its basic beliefs.

'That it is the opinion of this meeting that a society engaged in circulating the pure Word of God, and upon which devolves the responsibility of preparing and issuing new translations of the Holy Scriptures, must be considered decidedly a religious Society, and one that should be conducted on scriptural principles; and that those who are Protestants and acknowledge the scriptural doctrine of the Holy Trinity, can consistently, be admitted members of such a society, or be fit agents to conduct or carry on such a work.'

The following excerpts are from the laws and regulations also adopted at that meeting:

I. That this Society be designated the TRINITARIAN BIBLE SOCIETY.

II. The object of this Society is to promote the Glory of God and the salvation of men, by circulating, both at home and abroad, in dependence on the Divine Blessing, the HOLY SCRIPTURES, which are given by inspiration of God, and are able to make men wise unto salvation, through faith which is in Christ Jesus.

III. This Society shall circulate the HOLY SCRIPTURES, as comprised in the Canonical Books of the Old and New Testaments, WITHOUT NOTE

OR COMMENT, to the exclusion of the Apocrypha; the copies in the English Language shall be those of the authorized version....

IV. The MEMBERS of this Society shall consist of PROTESTANTS, who acknowledge their belief in the GODHEAD OF THE FATHER, OF THE SON, AND OF THE HOLY GHOST, THREE CO-EQUAL AND CO-ETERNAL PERSONS IN ONE LIVING AND TRUE GOD...

V. (Now XIII). This Society, acknowledging the ignorance and helplessness of man, deems it a bounden duty to express its entire dependence upon the Blessing of JEHOVAH, the FATHER, the SON, and the HOLY GHOST, in its "work of faith, and labour of love, and patience of hope," by offering up prayer and praise at all its meetings."

The Trinitarian Bible Society worked with English evangelicals while the British and Foreign Bible Society worked with Catholics, Modernists, and "soft" Protestants.

THE AMERICAN BIBLE SOCIETY

In 1816, the American Bible Society was formed. Its purpose was to make the Bible available to all the people of the world. It sponsored the distribution of the King James Bible throughout the United States and the translation and distribution of the Bible in the major languages of the world. All translations were to be made from the King James Bible.

In 1851, the American Bible Society produced a "revised" King James Bible. There was tremendous opposition for this decision among the members themselves.

Robert J. Beckinridge was a Presbyterian preacher and the president of Jefferson College in Philadelphia. He wrote against the new translation and helped organize opposition to it. He wrote:

> "It seemed to me that the time had fully come, for the friends of the Bible, as it is, to speak once more . . . Does anyone suppose that a question of conscience touching the integrity of the word of God, can be given up by Christian people even to avoid trouble in the church of God, much less trouble with a secular society? The Word of God is, next to the Spirit itself, the most precious gift of Christ to His church; and if the church has any clear duty upon earth, one duty is to preserve that Divine Word in purity. But here is a society purely secular and voluntary, having no function concerning the English Bible by its constitution or its character, but to circulate it; and here are its managers, its committee . . . and here is a new standard English Bible, changed . . . in somewhere about 24,000 particulars . . . we are told they have discovered . . . in the text and punctuation alone . . . And then they distinctly assert, that all of these 24,000 variations . . . 'there is not one which mars the integrity of the text, or affects any doctrine or precepts of the Bible' . . . the principle on which the procedure has been undertaken and carried through, are perilous in the highest degree . . . the results reached are evil, and only evil."

Episcopal preacher, A. Cleveland Coxe (famous for editing the publication of the Anti-Nicene, Nicene and Post-Nicene Fathers) also helped to organize the opposition to the new translation. In 1857, it was withdrawn.

Supporters of the new Bible withdrew from the ABS and formed a new Bible society to promote their New

English Bible. Sales were almost nonexistent and their new society withdrew publication. Again a new society was formed to promote a new English Bible and again it collapsed financially due to lack of sales.

By the 1870's, liberals and Roman Catholics were making great progress in the American Bible Society and the Bible believing members were no longer able to resist them. The American Bible Society began to actively endorse the idea of a new English Bible and the King James Bible was no longer the basis for foreign translations.

From the 1870's to the 1930's the American Bible Society produced a wide variety of types of translations. Some were from the Received Text, some were not. By the 1930's the Critical Text had complete dominance in all American Bible Society translation efforts.

THE FORMATION OF THE UNITED BIBLE SOCIETIES

In the 1930's, the British and Foreign Bible Society led most of the world's Bible societies into forming the United Bible Societies. The American Bible Society joined.

By now, the modernists were firmly in control. No Bible translation produced by a member of the United Bible Societies could be trusted to be faithful. Only a small handful of Bible Societies do not identify with the UBS. They include the Trinitarian Bible Society, the Graceway Bible Society (Canada) and the Russian Bible Society.

Most of the major languages had a good Bible translation. Some dated from the Reformation era; many had been produced by the Bible Societies in their earlier years. The purpose of most Bible Societies was now to replace these translations with translations of the Critical Text done by modernists. Often the United Bible Societies and American Bible Society owned copyrights for good Bible translations. Sometimes they used their copyright to prevent the printing of good Bibles. Good Bibles in languages like Korean, Norwegian, Japanese, Spanish and Portuguese were replaced with bad Bibles approved by modernists.

The United Bible Societies is at the heart of the modern ecumenical movement. Both the American Bible Society and the United Bible Societies are listed by the World Council of Churches as "Ecumenical Organizations Involved With the World Council of Churches" (see their Internet site).

A new generation of fundamentalists is rising up to challenge the control of the modernist Bible Societies over the translation and distribution of the Bible.

A good received text Portuguese Bible, translated by evangelicals is now available. An 1865 Received Text Spanish Bible has been reprinted. Other translation projects are underway in Spanish. Projects are underway in Norwegian, Korean, Japanese and other languages.

This is one of the great mission challenges of our new century. Will we burden millions of new Christians with translations of the Bible made by modernists?

Will we rise to the occasion and support legitimate translation efforts around the world?

DO YOU TRUST MODERNIST BIBLE SOCIETIES TO TRANSLATE THE BIBLE?

IS THE MODERN KING JAMES MOVEMENT THE PRODUCT OF THE SEVENTH DAY ADVENTIST CULT?

IS THE MODERN KING JAMES MOVEMENT THE PRODUCT OF THE SEVENTH DAY ADVENTIST CULT?

The wildest attack against King James Bible believers is that their position comes from the Seventh Day Adventist cult!

"All writers who embrace the KJV-only position have derived their views ultimately from Seventh-day Adventist missionary, theology professor, and college President, Benjamin G. Wilkinson (d. 1968) through one or two of his spiritual descendants."
-"Roots of the KJV Controversy"
Internet article by Doug Kuitlek

"So then Wilkinson, when he had conceived, brought forth Ray, and Ray, when he was full-grown brought forth Fuller, Ruckman, Waite, Chick, Riplinger, Hyles, Bynum, . . . "
-"Roots of the KJV Controversy"

"Some have described the "KJV only / Textus Receptus only" group as a cult. That half of a foundational book of the entire movement is the work of a leader in the Adventist Cult suggests that this description is correct."
-Gary Hudson, The Great Which Bible Fraud, Baptist Biblical Heritage, Summer 1990

In the book, From the Mind of God to the Mind of Man, J.B. Williams asserts that Benjamin Wilkinson is the "first notable deviation" from the position advocated in that book (p. 6).

Robert Joyner wrote: "Benjamin G. Wilkinson (died 1968), a Seventh Day Adventist, originated the King James Only view."

-King James Only, p. 34

THE FACTS

In his 1930 book, Our Authorized Bible Vindicated, Dr. Benjamin G. Wilkinson defended the text of the King James Bible and the underlying Greek and Hebrew texts upon which it was based. In a clear and cogent way he demonstrated that these were the texts used by many independent churches throughout the centuries.

Large sections of Wilkinson's book were reprinted in 1970 by David Otis Fuller in his book Which Bible.

Wilkinson was a professor of theology at a Seventh Day Adventist college. He does not identify himself as a Seventh Day Adventist in his book. He was later the President of a Seventh Day Adventist college. Dr. Fuller did not identify him as a Seventh Day Adventist when he reprinted his work.

WILKINSON'S CONTRIBUTION!

The arguments of Kuitlek, Hudson, Williams and others distort the situation. First, there is nothing new or original in Wilkinson's book (I have a copy). His historical arguments are a restatement of Frederick Nolan's An Inquiry into the Integrity of the Greek Vulgate or Received Text of the New Testament, published in 1815. The same arguments about church history are seen in the writings of R.L. Dabney and Louis Gaussen in the 1800's and before that in the writings of John Calvin and Francis Turretin. His refutation of Westcott and Hort had already been made by Dean John Burgon, Edward Miller and F.A. Scrivener. His doctrinal arguments about the Scripture had already been made by a number of Church of England, Lutheran, Calvinist and Baptist preachers and writers.

To declare that Wilkinson taught something new about the doctrine of Scripture or the history of the text is to declare yourself ignorant of hundreds of years of debate about the doctrine of Scripture and the history of the transmission of the text.

Wilkinson's only contribution to the study of the history of the Bible was to take Nolan's 500 page argument about the history of the Bible and present it in 250 pages.

Second, there is nothing uniquely Seventh Day Adventist about Wilkinson's position concerning the Bible. This position about the Bible is not the position of the Seventh Day Adventist movement. It is not the position of any influential writer or leader among the Seventh Day Adventists. Dr. Wilkinson was writing for himself, not for the cult of which he was a member. Simply put, one heretical Bible teacher discovered for himself an accurate history of the transmission of the Bible. He tried to call his cult to a recognition of the issue. Apparently, very few listened. The SDA still publishes Wilkinson's other book, Truth Triumphant but has no plans to republish Our Authorized Bible Vindicated (verified in a phone call, November 3, 2003). Others, outside of the SDA, came to appreciate his clear and well documented statement of historical facts.

Thirdly, not everything believed by every cultist is wrong. Seventh Day Adventist founder, Ellen G. White, wrote criticizing the Roman Catholic church for persecuting independent churches. Wilkinson is attacked for quoting her about the persecution of independent preachers by Roman Catholic authorities. But the fact that Seventh Day

Adventists refer to this historical incident does not change the fact that this is real history.

The fact that one Seventh Day Adventist wrote about the history of the transmission of the Bible does not change the facts of the transmission of the Bible. The Seventh Day Adventists have produced some excellent materials refuting evolution. Does this mean that the entire creationist movement is simply the product of the Seventh Day Adventist cult? If you followed the logic of Kuitlek, Hudson, Williams, and Joyner, you would be forced to reject creationism.

DO YOU REALLY WANT TO START MAKING COMPARISONS WITH THE SEVENTH DAY ADVENTISTS?

Wilkinson was never successful in influencing the Seventh Day Adventists to adopt his position on the text or translation of the Bible or on the King James Bible. In fact, the official positions of the Seventh Day Adventist cult about the text and translation of the Bible are the same as the positions of Doug Kuitlek, Gary Hudson, J.B. Williams, and Robert Joyner. The SDA shares the same position about the Bible that you would find in From the Mind of God to the Mind of Man.

In fact, if you would really like to read a spirited defense of the Westcott and Hort Theory read the publications of the Jehovah's Witness and the Theosophy cult. Does this mean that all the modern proponents of the Westcott and Hort Theory got their doctrine from Charles Taze Russell and Helen Blavatsky? Of course not!

CONCLUSION

Benjamin Wilkinson writes: "Unitarians and Romanizers may serve to revise the Bible for others, but not for evangelical Protestants." In making this statement he was just repeating the position stated by the Trinitarian Bible Society in 1831. In this position he shows more wisdom than those who accuse him of inventing new ideas.

IN DEFENSE OF MARK 16:9-20

IN DEFENSE OF MARK 16:9-20

"It is easy to join the critics and say Mark's original manuscript ended with verse 8, it is impossible to satisfactorily support this statement."

-Dean John Burgon

IS IT OR ISN'T IT?

Many modern evangelical "scholars" find themselves unsure of whether Mark 16:9-20 is really part of the Bible.

Many Bible students have puzzled over the note about Mark 16:9-20 in the Old Scofield Reference Bible. This note reads, "The passage from verse 9 to the end is not found in the two most ancient manuscripts, the Sinatic and Vatican, and others have it with partial omissions and variations. But it is quoted by Irenaeus and Hippolytus in the second or third century."

Can you imagine the confusion that a young Christian has when they read this note? Does this mean that it is to be considered as spurious or is there a reason to trust this passage? The Scofield Reference Bible raised the question, but never answered it!

Many evangelical preachers seem sure that it makes no difference at all. The King James has the passage but the NIV rejects it as Scripture. Many evangelicals will assure you that the NIV and the King James are so much the same that it doesn't make any difference which one you use.

But if you believe in the verbal inspiration of Scripture, every word matters. We are forbidden to add to Scripture and we are forbidden to subtract from Scripture. (Revelation 22:18-19) **Either someone committed a**

terrible act by trying to remove eleven verses of precious Scripture from the Bible or someone perpetrated a horrible fraud by trying to add eleven verses written by men to the Bible. You can't have it both ways. Things that are different are not the same.

Some evangelical scholars are not so indecisive. They are sure that Mark 16:9-20 is spurious:

> A.T. Robertson, Studies in Mark - "It is possible that the last leaf of Mark was lost before any copies were made of it. If Mark did write more of his gospel (after verse 8)and if copies were made of the autograph before it perished, then some day we may see the true ending of Mark's Gospel."

> Howard F. Vos, A Study Guide Commentary - "The very best manuscripts stop at verse 8. The great scholar Eusebius, writing in the 4th century, said that nearly all copies of Mark's Gospel ended in verse 8. Jerome said almost the same thing. Many argue that verses 9-20 are not in the same style as the rest of the Book, so the tendency of modern textual scholars is to omit these verses."

> Tyndale, NT Commentary - "Verses 9-20 are not found in some important witnesses. This longer ending shows knowledge of John 20, Luke 24 and Matthew 28. This is an early attempt to 'round off' a Gospel whose original ending has become in some way maimed or lost. These verses were perhaps derived from the other Gospels, a patchwork of pieces from the other Gospels."

THE ARGUMENTS FOR REJECTING MARK 16:9-20

Argument Number One!
Mark 16:9-20 is not found in the two manuscripts, Sinaticus and Vaticanus, that Westcott and Hort (and most modern critics) put their faith in. These two manuscripts serve as the primary authority for many of the "scholars" of the evangelical world.

Argument Number Two!
Eusebius, church historian for Constantine and devoted disciple of Origen, wrote about the ending of Mark 16. He challenged the integrity of the long ending and declared that he used texts without this ending. His work was acknowledged by Jerome. Some have claimed that this was an endorsement on Jerome's part, but he clearly acknowledged Mark 16:9-20 as Scripture. He simply stated that such texts as Eusebius referred to existed. The debate over Mark 16 is not a new one.

Argument Number Three!
Some scholars claim that the style of Mark 16:9-20 is too different from the rest of the book of Mark. There are some words found in Mark 16:9-20 that are not found in the rest of the book.

The reading of the overwhelming majority of the manuscripts of the book of Mark have been rejected based upon these three arguments.

CRITICAL ENDINGS

So how do the modern textual critics believe that Mark 16 should end? The more theologically modernist critics usually believe that verse 8 is the real ending of Mark. For them the last words of Mark are "for they were afraid."

A few "scholars" and some cults accept a short ending for Mark which was found in one Latin manuscript.

Many "evangelical scholars" believe that the original ending of Mark has been lost. They hope that it may be found again some day. In their thinking God inspired the "originals" but He never promised to preserve His word. They have no problem with the idea that the genuine God-given ending for Mark has been lost and is currently not available. Not only do they not have a problem with this position—they seem to take real comfort in it. (See the author's booklet, The Scripture Cannot Be Broken)

If the God-given ending of Mark is lost then that pesky doctrine of preservation is "done away with" and "scholars" have become the final authority for believers today.

VARIOUS VERSIONS AND MARK 16

The RSV

The Revised Standard Version has a note that says that Mark 16:9-20 is not found "in some manuscripts."

It also offers an alternate two verse ending which reads, "v 9-10 The women quickly told Peter and his friends what had happened. Later, Jesus sent the disciples to the east and to the west with his sacred and everlasting message of how people can be saved forever."

The Philips New Testament

J.B. Philips translates the verses, but he provides a heading that lists them as "an ancient appendix" to the book of Mark.

The New World Translation
The Jehovah's Witness translation provides both the long and short endings to Mark 16 with notes that explain that both have some support in "certain manuscripts."

The Williams New Testament
Williams provides a note that says verse 8 ends the book of Mark in the two best manuscripts.

The Beck New Testament
The New Testament in the Language of Today (Beck) provides a note at verse 8 that says "The two oldest and best manuscripts do not have Mark 16:9-20 but end Mark's Gospel with verse 8."

The Living Bible
The Living Bible provides a note at verse 8 that reads, "Verse 9-20 are not found in the most ancient manuscripts but may be considered an appendix giving additional facts."

The Weymouth Translation
Weymouth provides brackets around verses 9-20.

The Moffat Translation
Dr. Moffat adds a footnote that says the reader has a choice of two endings—each an appendix written in the second century attempting to complete what Mark left undone.

The NEB
The New English Bible provides a note after verse 8 that reads, "At this point some of the most ancient witnesses bring the book to a close."

The NASV
The New American Standard Version prints verse 9-20 in brackets and provides a note that reads "Some of the oldest manuscripts omit verse 9-20."

The NIV
The New International Version places this note between verse 8 and verse 9. "The most reliable early manuscripts and other ancient witnesses do not have Mark 16:9-20."

The New King James Bible provides this note at the end of verse 20, "Verses 9-20 are bracketed in Nu-Texts as not original. They are lacking in Codex Sinaticus and Codes Vaticanus, although **nearly all other manuscripts of Mark contain them.**"

THE MANUSCRIPT EVIDENCE FOR MARK 16:9-20

Of the five manuscripts that Westcott and Hort considered the oldest, two (Vaticanus and Sinaticus) do not contain Mark 16:9-20. The other three do contain this passage.

Of the next fifteen manuscripts generally considered the oldest all fifteen contain the full ending of Mark.

Out of 600 minuscule manuscripts, all 600 contain Mark 16:9-20, 618 out of 620 manuscripts often considered most important by most evangelical scholars contain Mark 16:9-20.

These verses are found in all ancient Latin copies of the book of Mark except one.

The earliest ancient translations, Latin, Gothic and Coptic all include these verses. Among the Syrian translations, all but one (the Siniatic Syriac) contains this passage.

QUOTATIONS FROM ANCIENT CHURCH LEADERS AND ORGANIZATIONS

These verses were quoted as Scripture by many church leaders. Some of these quotes were made 150 years before Sinaticus and Vaticanus were produced.

Justin Martyr (AD 150), Irenaeus (AD180), Tation (AD 170), and Hippolytus (AD 250) all quote Mark 16:9-20 as Scripture.

Jerome (AD 331-420) acknowledges that some people were using Greek manuscripts that don't contain Mark 16:9-20. However, he quotes it ias Scripture and included this passage in his Latin Vulgate translation.

Augustine (AD 395-430) quotes these verses as Scripture often. So do Nestorious (AD 430), Cyril of Alexandria (AD 444), and Hesychius of Jerusalem (AD430).

Victor of Antioch (AD 425-450) stated that the last few verses of Mark had been deliberately omitted by certain copyists. He was clear that there was no good reason for this but some teachers omitted them because they wanted to. He pointed out that the vast majority of manuscripts contained these verses and that he was convinced that they were genuine.

Lectionaries in common use among Eastern and Western churches routinely contained Mark 16:9-20. This is true in lectionaries used by Catholic, Orthodox, Monophysite and Gothic churches. Mark 16:9-20 was also routinely used in church liturgies among all different professing Christian groups.

THE ABSURDITY OF AN ABRUPT ENDING AT MARK 16:8

To end Mark 16 at verse 8, with no account of the resurrection and the disciples trembling in fear, destroys any meaningful purpose for the book. Even liberal textual critic J.J. Griesbach wrote:

"No one can imagine that Mark cut short the thread of his narrative so ineptly."

Evangelical Bible teacher, Arno Gabelein wrote:

"Higher criticism declares that the proper ending of the Gospel of Mark is verse 8. They disputed the genuineness of verses 9-20. Another hand, they claim, added later these verses. That spurious translation, which goes under the name of The Twentieth Century New Testament (wholly unsatisfactory), also gives this portion as 'a late appendix.' It is not. Mark wrote it and some of the best scholars have declared that it is genuine. How foolish to assume that the blessed document, which begins with the sublime statement 'The gospel of Jesus Christ, the Son of God' could end with 'they were afraid!' The trouble with these critics is that they approach the Word of God with doubt and reject its inspiration."

G. Campbell Morgan, J. Vernon McGee, R.H. Lenski, Bruce McClaren, and Albert Barnes have all written refuting the liberal attempt to end Mark 16 with verse 8.

WHAT ABOUT THE ARGUMENT CONCERNING WRITING STYLE?

Liberals are always reflecting on the possibility that the style of writing of some passages prove that it wasn't written by just one author. They tell us Deuteronomy was written by four authors and that Isaiah was finished by Deutero-Isaiah. They tell us that Daniel was a compilation and that Paul couldn't have written Ephesians. They assure us that different men wrote I and II Peter. They speculate that the John of the Gospel of John and the John of the book of Revelation are different men.

However their arguments are always subjective and personal. They believe these things simply because they want to!

In 1946 R.H. Lenski wrote five pages about the arguments concerning literary style and the ending of Mark 16. He demolished the arguments of the liberals. He pointed out that every chapter of the book of Mark contains at least one word that is unique to that chapter. Liberals reject the ending of Mark 16 over the issue of literary style for one reason – they want to!

THE STRANGE BLANK IN THE VATICANUS MANUSCRIPT

Following Mark 16:8 in the Vaticanus manuscript (one of the two authorities for rejecting Mark 16:9-20) there is a blank space of 42 empty lines before Luke 1 begins. This is the only blank area in the entire 759-page manuscript.

Dean John Burgon comments on the importance of this unusual blank space:

"The older manuscript from which Codex B was copied must have infallibly contained the twelve verses in dispute. The copyist was instructed to leave a blank space in memoriam rei. Never was blank more intelligible! Never was silence more eloquent!

By this simple expedient, strange to relate, the Vatican Codex is made to recite itself even while it seems to be bearing testimony against the concluding verses of St. Mark's Gospel, by withholding them: for it forbids the inference which, under ordinary circumstances, must have been drawn from that omission.

It does more. By leaving room for the verses it omits, it brings into prominent notice at the end of fifteen centuries and a half, a more ancient witness than itself. The venerable author of the original codex from which Codex B was copied, is thereby besought to view. And thus, our supposed adversary (Codex B) proves our most useful ally; for it procures us the testimony of an hitherto unsuspected witness. The earlier scribe unmistakably comes forward at this stage of inquiry, to explain that he at least is prepared to answer for the genuineness of these twelve concluding verses with which the later scribe, his copyist, from his omission of them, might unhappily be thought to have been unacquainted."

-Fuller, Counterfeit or Genuine, p. 67-68

N. CLAYTON CROY

In 2003 N. Clayton Croy's book, *The Mutilation of Mark's Gospel*, was published. It is a compendium of all the different views of the ending of Mark.

He considers the rejection of Mark 16:9-20 by Westcott and Hort as proof that these verses do not belong in the Bible. For him, clearly Sinaticus and Vaticanus are authoritative, p.21.

He admits that the vast majority of all manuscripts contain the traditional ending and that it was accepted throughout the centuries, p.19.

He completely refutes the idea that Mark 16 could have ended at verse 8. However, since he is sure that the Traditional Text and the King James Bible couldn't possibly be right, he concludes that the true ending of Mark 16 must be lost. Since he doesn't believe in the doctrine of preservation this is not a problem for him.

He approvingly quotes the statement of Fenton Hort about Mark 16:9-20:

> "There is . . . no difficulty in supposing . . . (1) that the true intended continuation of vv. 1-8 either was very early lost by the detachment of a leaf or was never written down; and (2) that a scribe or editor, unwilling to change the words of the text before him or to add words of his own, was willing to furnish the gospel with what seemed a worthy conclusion by incorporating with it unchanged a narrative of Christ's appearance after the Resurrection which he found in some secondary record then surviving from a preceding generation. If these suppositions are made, the whole tenour of the evidence becomes clear and harmonious. Every other view is, we believe, untenable."
> -Westcott and Hort, *The New Testament in the Original Greek*, p. 46

Hort was not bound by any belief in divine preservation of Scripture.

"WHAT ABOUT DIVINE PRESERVATION?"

David Otis Fuller, in his introduction to Burgon's *The Last Twelve Verses of Mark* writes:

> "Every faithful Christian must reckon seriously with the teaching of Christ concerning the providential preservation of Scripture. Our Lord evidently believed that the Old Testament Scriptures had been preserved in their original purity from the time of their first writing down to His own day and that this providential preservation would continue until the end of the ages."

Are the last verses of Mark lost? If they are, is there any more Scripture lost? Can anyone be sure that we are not missing passages from every other book? If Mark 16:9-20 is spurious, is our Bible full of other false passages?

Your perspective will be determined by your doctrine. The evidence for Mark 16:9-20 is overwhelming. But if you are determined to protect Vaticanus or Sinaticus you just won't face the evidence. If you are determined to protect Westcott and Hort you will find it easy to reject the evidence. If you are determined not to admit that you and your fellow "scholars" are wrong about one of your fundamentally important beliefs then you will claim that you can't find one verse in the Bible about divine preservation – so it is no problem if the ending of Mark is lost.

If you trust what the Bible says about divine preservation you will find it easy to face the facts of history and the overwhelming manuscript evidence for Mark 16:9-20.

WHY MAINTAIN THE ATTACK ON MARK 16:9-20?

The evidence for the genuineness of Mark 16:9-20 is compelling. So why do so many cling to the discredited attacks against Mark 16:9-20?

Modernists desperately cling to the idea that Mark 16 ends with verse 8. This is important to them. They deny the essence of the Christian faith (the bodily resurrection of Christ), but they want to be accepted within Christianity anyway. If you end Mark 16 at verse 8 there is no account of the resurrection in Mark 16. Liberals claim that Mark shared their doubts about the resurrection. If you recognize Mark 16:9-20 as Scripture their argument is finished.

Many "evangelical scholars" also have a vested interest in denying Mark 16:9-20. For almost one hundred years, "evangelical scholarship" has accepted the idea that the Sinaticus and the Vaticanus manuscripts are the "older and better manuscripts." This has become a fundamental of the faith for many modern evangelicals. If you do not believe this you are rejected as an unscholarly, unsound fanatic. You are dismissed as "a simpleton."

Every day in the classrooms of the vast majority of evangelical (and independent Baptist) Bible colleges and seminaries, the Traditional Text and the King James Bible is corrected based upon the authority of the Sinaticus and Vaticanus texts. Commentaries have been published which cover every verse by correcting the King James reading with the older and better manuscripts.

In the matter of the ending of the book of Mark, these manuscripts disagree dramatically with the Majority Text (Textus Receptus, Byzantine Text). They also disagree with the vast majority of other Alexandrian texts. Their approach to the ending of Mark is virtually unique. On this matter, they are either the very best of all texts or the very worst.

In his article, *The Secret Spanking of Westcott and Hort*, Dean Burgon makes this point. These two manuscripts are either the very closest to the originals that we have or the ones that are the farthest away. Things that are different are not the same!

If we face the facts about Mark 16:9-20 we must admit that these two texts are inferior. If that is true then the very foundation for teaching the Bible in most of our colleges and seminaries has been false for almost a century. Pride won't allow many to make that admission, no matter what the facts are.

If Mark 16:9-20 was given by God, then many modern "evangelical scholars" are found to be less than scholarly. Their criticism of the Traditional Text has for years been based upon a false premise. Their agreement with unsaved textual critics about the text of the Bible is found to be unsound.

A PERSONAL TESTIMONY

I was saved in 1963 as a ten-year-old. I was a "bus kid" attending a non-denominational church in inner-city Indianapolis. My Sunday school teacher taught me that the Bible was the Word of God. Every word of it! I accepted it, including Mark 16:9-20, without question.

When I was seventeen, I surrendered to the call to preach. By this time, I was attending an independent Baptist Church. Our church recommended that everyone use an Old Scofield Reference Bible. I requested one for Christmas and my mother bought me one. Imagine my surprise to discover that I John 5:7 was not inspired and that Mark 16:9-20 was questionable.

I attended four years of Bible College and never heard the text issue or the Bible debate discussed. This subject was so completely ignored that I now wonder if the professors were instructed to ignore it to avoid controversy!

After graduating from college I found myself teaching a Sunday School class on the book of Mark. I carefully studied all the commentaries available to me. Almost all agreed that Mark 16:9-20 was spurious. I wanted to be a serious student and share the best scholarship with my Sunday School students. However, I couldn't get peace about telling them that the King James ending of Mark was false. I ignored the subject and taught through Mark 16:9-20, but I felt guilty about it!

A number of years later, I began a serious historical study of the different text types underlying the various translations of the New Testament. I realized how shallow the phrase "older and better manuscripts" is. If a corrupted copy of Mark 16 was made the day after God gave the original, and if we found that copy today, it would be the oldest copy of a part of the N.T. ever found. It would be "older and more corrupt." I realized that "modern evangelical scholarship" was based upon "theological political correctness" and not on history, reason and evidence.

I accepted the Traditional Text and the King James Bible by faith. I now had the same view of the Bible I had when I was a bus kid! I believed every word of the Bible that God was using. I had come full circle.

I am still fascinated by the arguments that people use for rejecting the Textus Receptus and King James readings. I am amazed at how history, reason and logic are consistently ignored in the attempt to be considered "scholarly" (theologically correct). I now understand why the Textus Receptus and the King James Bible has withstood all of the attacks of the centuries and why they have survived unscathed.

I now teach Mark 16:9-20 as the absolute, verbally inspired Word of God without any question or guilt. The evidence will always support the Scripture if we are not blinded by our desire to be accepted by men who don't accept the Scriptures.

In 1907 the Freer Manuscript (now known as Codex W) was discovered in Egypt. It dates back to the fourth century. It contains Mark 16:9-20 with wording exactly like that of the Traditional Text.

Samuel Zwemer, *The Last Twelve Verses of the Gospel of Mark*, 1918, writes:

> "After all this we are content to turn to the text of the authorized English version, to scores of translations

made by the Bible Societies into hundreds of languages and rejoice to find in them no break and no mutilation of the Mark text."

I wonder how many thousands of bus kids today understand Mark 16:9-20 better than many of our independent Baptist seminary professors.

About the Author

Phil Stringer, Ph.D., is the pastor of the Ravenswood Baptist Church of Chicago. He is a former Bible college president.

He is an active Bible conference speaker having spoken at over 380 churches, camps and schools. He has spoken in 46 states and 13 countries.

He is a visiting professor at Landmark Baptist College (Manila, Philippines), Asia Baptist Bible College, (Manila, Philippines), Dayspring Bible College (Lake Zurich, Illinois), Westwood Baptist School of Missions (Winter Haven, Florida), and the Florida Baptist College (Tampa, Florida). He often teaches as a guest lecturer at other schools. He has taught courses at 16 colleges.

He has written 4 books, 16 booklets, 22 college curriculums, 5 high school curriculums and 1 elementary school curriculum.

He serves on the Board of Directors of Heritage Baptist College, the King James Bible Research Council and the American Association of Bible College Educators. He serves on the Advisory Boards for Bible Nation, Shalom Native Mission, The Dean Burgon Society, and the Graceway Bible Society. He is the President of the William Carey Bible Society.

He graduated with a Bachelor of Science in Bible degree from Indiana Baptist College in 1975. He received a Masters degree in Christian Education from Freedom University in 1980. He received a Doctor of Philosophy degree in English Bible from Landmark Baptist College in 1997. He received a Doctor of Religious Education degree from the American Bible College in 2004.

Dr. Stringer was awarded the honorary degree of Doctor of Divinity by the Asia Baptist Bible College in 2002. He was awarded the honorary degree of Doctor of Literature by the American Bible College in 2002. In 2007, he was awarded the Heritage Baptist University Alumni educator of the year award. In 2008, he received the Hoosier Hills Baptist Camp pastor of the year award.

He can be contacted at:

5846 N. Kimball,
Chicago, IL 60659
Phone: (773) 478-6083
Email: philstringer@att.net

BOOKS AND DVDS AVAILABLE FROM DR. PHIL STRINGER

$3.00 Books

Majestic Legacy—a look at the 400-year legacy of the King James Bible. The impact of the King James Bible on politics, literature, linguistics, culture and revival.

Biblical English—the distinctive English necessary to convey the original Greek and Hebrew Scriptures into English.

History of the English Bible—the record of the transmission of the Bible into the English language.

In Defense of I John—the most attacked verse in the Bible is I John 5:7. The reasons for including this verse in the text of Scripture are given.

Misidentified Identity—a refutation of the cultic heresies of the Christian Identity movement.

The Real Story of King James—a refutation of the false

ABOUT THE AUTHOR

charges of homosexuality made against King James I.

The Westcott and Hort Only Theory—a refutation of the theory that has challenged the Traditional Text and exerted so much influence on the religious world today.

The Means of Inspiration—a Biblical and historical study proving that the Holy Spirit dictated the words of Scripture.

Many Infallible Proofs—Biblical and historical proof of the existence of Christ and his bodily resurrection.

The Real Story—a look at the missed lessons of history from the Nazis, St. Patrick and others.

Fifty Demonstrations of America's Christian Heritage—fifty proofs of the impact of Biblical Christianity on the development of the culture of the United States.

The Received Text for the Whole World—the importance of having a Received Text based translation for every language of the world.

Ready Answers—an answer to several criticisms of the King James Bible that are advanced by evangelicals and fundamentalists.

The DaVinci Code Controversy—a refutation of the religious and historical themes of the popular books and movies.

$10 DVDs

The History of the English Bible—the history of the Bible from the giving of Scripture to the King James Bible. Originally given at the University of Michigan.

Majestic Legacy—two messages on the 400-year impact of the King James Bible. Originally given at the Immanuel Baptist Church of Corona, Michigan.

$8.00 Book

The Messianic Claims of Gail Riplinger—a refutation of

READY ANSWERS

Gail Riplinger's claims to being a modern-day prophetess.

$12 Books

The Faithful Baptist Witness—a look at the doctrines and history of the historic Baptist movement. A history designed for the average person in the pew.

Gail Riplinger's Occult Connections—a look at the occult teachings of Gail Riplinger's that have infiltrated Baptist churches.

All of these materials may be ordered from:
Dr. Phil Stringer
5846 N. Kimball Ave.
Chicago, IL 60659
philstringer@att.net
All orders above $25.00 are postpaid.

Dr. Stringer is available to speak at conferences on any of the topics covered in his books. Usually this is done on a two-day basis on a Monday and Tuesday. At times, other schedules can be arranged.